O c e a n
Ecosystems

by ELLEN HALLORAN

Table of Contents

CHAPTER 1

Earth's Oceans

Of all the planets in the solar system, only Earth has a surface covered mostly with water. Saltwater oceans cover about 71 percent of Earth's surface. As a result, the oceans receive two thirds of all the Sun's heat that reaches Earth. Water near the equator gets more of this heat than water near the poles. There are four major oceans on Earth. They are the Pacific Ocean, the Atlantic Ocean, the Indian Ocean, and the Arctic Ocean.

PACIFIC OCEAN

ATLANTIC OCEAN

The Pacific is Earth's largest ocean. It covers about 45 percent of Earth's water area and about one third of Earth's surface. It is larger than the world's total land area. The deepest place in all the oceans is in the Pacific Ocean, near Japan. It is called the Marianas Trench. A trench is a deep valley in the ocean floor. The Marianas Trench is 11 kilometers (7 miles) deep.

The Atlantic is the second-largest ocean. It covers 25 percent of Earth's water area. It is home to many of the species of fish that people eat. However, in the twentieth century, people took hundreds of millions of tons of fish and shellfish from the waters of the Atlantic Ocean.

This photograph of Earth was taken from space.

ARCTIC OCEAN

PACIFIC OCEAN

INDIAN OCEAN

The leatherback sea turtle, found in the Indian Ocean, is the largest living reptile.

The Indian Ocean has about 21 percent of Earth's water area. This ocean is home to many sea creatures, such as sharks, dolphins, and leatherback sea turtles.

The Arctic Ocean is the smallest of the major oceans. Still, it is about 14 million square kilometers (5.4 million square miles) in area. That is one-and-a-half times the size of the United States. In winter, most of the Arctic Ocean is covered by ice.

More than 99 percent of living space on Earth is in our oceans. Our oceans have many different **ecosystems.** Let's explore some of them.

Ice is Nice!

Some people refer to the ocean surrounding the ice-covered continent of Antarctica as the Antarctic Ocean, or the Southern Ocean. The word *Antarctica* means "opposite to the Arctic." The Arctic region surrounds the North Pole. Antarctica surrounds the South Pole.

The Southern Ocean is actually made up of the southern parts of the Atlantic, Pacific, and Indian Oceans. More than 50 percent of this ocean freezes over in winter. In summer it is home to sea lions and whales.

Emperor penguins are the only large animals that live in Antarctica year-round.

CHAPTER 2

Coral Reefs

Orange
cup coral

Great Barrier Reef, in Queensland, Australia,
is the largest coral reef in the world.

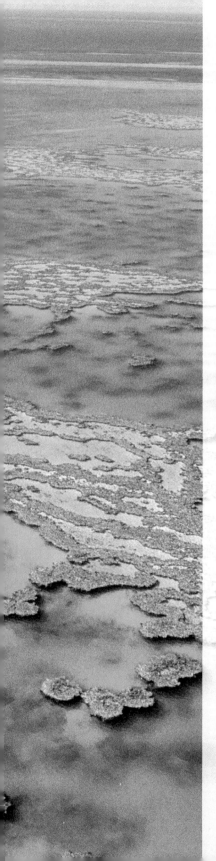

Coral reefs are one kind of ocean ecosystem. Most coral reefs are found in warm waters near the equator. The Pacific has more coral reefs than any other ocean.

Tiny, soft-bodied animals, called coral polyps, build reefs. Most polyps depend on algae living within their bodies for food. The algae change the Sun's energy into food through **photosynthesis**. Because algae need sunlight, most coral reefs do not grow below 60 meters (200 feet).

Coral polyps use their mouth and tentacles to get food. They eat small prey. They also eat organisms (living things) that drift in the water. These organisms are called **plankton**.

A coral polyp uses minerals from seawater to build a protective skeleton of calcium around its soft body. When a polyp dies, its skeleton remains. Other polyps build on that skeleton to form a coral reef.

Coral reefs cover less than one percent of the oceans. Yet they are home to nearly 25 percent of all marine fish. This ecosystem contains many different plants and animals. Many **invertebrates**, such as lobsters, sponges, and clams, find shelter in the reefs. Sharks, manta rays, and barracudas swim through these reefs searching for prey.

The sea anemone (uh-NE-muh-nee) is one of the animals living in the coral reef. It is an invertebrate with a tube-shaped body covered by many stinging tentacles. The anemone looks like a flower. It uses its tentacles to poison the small fish it uses for food—except for the clownfish.

Coral reefs are home to nearly 25 percent of all marine fish.

The clownfish and the sea anemone have an interesting relationship. The clownfish feeds on parasites that can harm or eat the anemone. The clownfish has a special coating on its body that protects it from the anemone's poisons. At night, when the anemone curls up, it makes a safe place for the clownfish to sleep.

Coral reefs are in danger. They are threatened by pollution, damage from ships, and careless divers. These reefs are also threatened by people who break off pieces of coral to collect or sell as souvenirs.

Clownfish swimming among sea anemone

CHAPTER 3

The Continental Shelf

A **continental shelf** is the underwater extension of
a continent. It slopes gently down from the
shore to a depth of about 182 meters (600 feet).
Eighty-one kilometers (50 miles) from shore, the land
plunges steeply downward to form the continental
slope. At the base of the slope is the continental rise.
It is a build-up of sand and mud. The continental rise
stretches from the slope to the floor of the ocean.

The continental shelf is mostly flat. In some places it is narrow, and in others it is hundreds of kilometers wide. Although the shelf makes up only 8 percent of the ocean's surface area, it holds 90 percent of the world's catch of fish and seafood. It is packed with the bulk of the ocean's plant life.

Why is this ecosystem so rich in plant and animal life? The continental shelf has a great supply of nutrients. Rivers, streams, and rainwater runoff carry minerals, silt, and organic matter to the shelf. Sunlight easily penetrates its shallow water. Plants use the Sun's energy to produce food for themselves and for the animals that eat these plants.

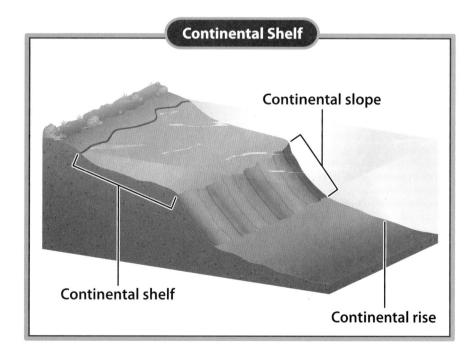

Continental Shelf

Continental slope

Continental shelf

Continental rise

An anemone crab is usually found in the tentacles of a sea anemone.

The oceans are filled with tiny living things called plankton. Many are so small that they can be seen only with a microscope. Examples of plankton are microscopic algae, newly hatched fish, crabs, and jellyfish. Large schools of fish feed on plankton. Lobsters, scallops, oysters, and some fish eat food that sinks from the surface and collects on the bottom of the continental shelf. The bottom also gives young fish places to hide from predators.

Currents are streams of water that flow through the ocean. They are important to the continental shelf ecosystem. Surface currents carry warm water and move the Sun's heat a long way. Deep currents carry cold water. Currents affect the climate of the land and keep it from being too hot or too cold.

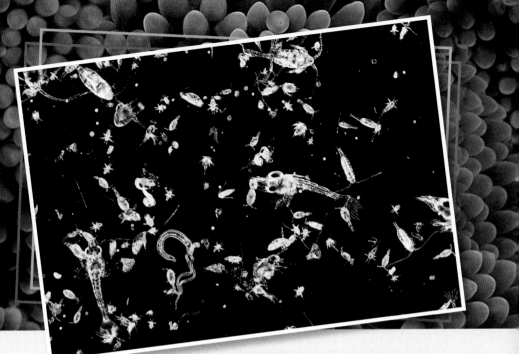

Plankton are very tiny plants and animals that float in the ocean.

In some areas, streams of cold water from deeper parts of the ocean move across the continental shelf. This movement brings up nutrients that have settled on the ocean floor. These cold currents mix with the continental shelf's warm, shallow water. Bottom feeders such as scallops, cod, and haddock thrive on the nutrients brought up from the ocean floor.

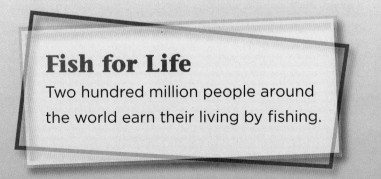

Fish for Life
Two hundred million people around the world earn their living by fishing.

CHAPTER 4

The Deep Sea

Alvin, a deep-
sea exploration
vehicle, has
allowed scientists

The deep sea is a very cold and dark place. The weight of the water produces a great deal of pressure. It is not a welcoming place for divers. Yet many animals are able to live in this ecosystem. In fact, this unexplored part of the oceans is the largest habitat, or living place, on Earth.

Sunlight reaches only the top 198 meters (650 feet) of water in the ocean. A smaller amount of sunlight reaches the midwater zone down to about 1,000 meters (3,280 feet). Below this is a zone of nearly total darkness. This zone goes down to 8,000 meters (26,250 feet).

Animals living in this sunless ecosystem have developed some interesting **adaptations**. All deep-sea fish are carnivores, or meat-eaters. Many have long, sharp teeth. Other deep-sea fish have large mouths and stomachs that expand to help them swallow animals that are bigger than they are. Some fish can stretch their mouths to ten times the size of their bodies!

All deep-sea fish, such as this fangtooth, are carnivores, or meat-eaters.

The deep sea looks much the same at similar depths in any of the world's oceans. It is when we move vertically (up and down) in the water that we note the greatest differences.

Since sufficient sunlight reaches only the top 198 meters (650 feet) of water, almost all ocean plants grow in this upper zone. It is here that plants use light to make their food through photosynthesis.

At night, billions of deep-sea animals rise to the surface waters to feed on plankton and tiny animals. At dawn, they travel back down to the darker water to hide from predators. This up-and-down journey is called *vertical migration*. It is the largest daily movement of life on Earth.

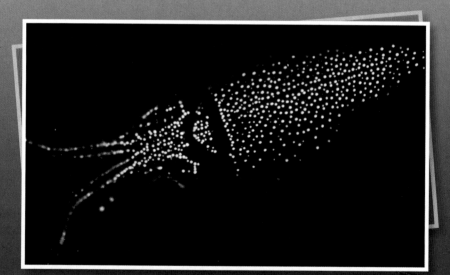

The firefly squid uses light to attract its prey.

When the animals migrate downward, they bring surface nutrients to the predators that feed on them. Other food that becomes available in the darkness includes dead plankton, animal carcasses, and drifting organic matter.

Below 914 meters (3,000 feet), 90 percent of deep-sea animals can release light. This adaptation helps them find food and mates. It also allows them to avoid enemies. A chemical reaction inside the animal's body releases energy in the form of light. Most of the light appears blue. Blue light travels very quickly underwater.

This comb jelly (above) and squid (below) are examples of deep-sea fish that release energy in the form of light.

This deep-sea anglerfish has a "fishing rod" on top of its head. Millions of bacteria cause the rod to light up and attract smaller fish.

Some animals use bright flashes of light to confuse enemies. Others squirt clouds of light-filled particles to distract their predators as they sneak away. At times, the deep sea looks like a starry night sky.

Some deep-sea fish have developed body parts that look like small animals or pieces of food. These parts can appear on a fish's tail, back, or head. The fish use them to attract other animals. Then they grab the animal and eat it.

Other deep-sea adaptations include large eyes to capture the little light that is available. Some animals have eyes that are thirty times more sensitive to light than human eyes!

The large habitat of the deep sea is the least-explored ecosystem on Earth. The pressure and cold temperatures found deep in the ocean make it difficult for scientists to investigate. Scientists are developing new tools to learn more about life in the deepest, darkest part of the ocean.

The Crowd Beneath the Waves

One creature of the deep sea is the rattail fish. There are 20 billion of them. That is more than three times the number of people on Earth!

CHAPTER 5

The Ocean Floor

Strike It Rich!

Mountains on the ocean floor have billions of tons of minerals, such as copper, zinc, silver, and gold.

An underwater observatory, HUGO, monitors the Loihi volcano on the ocean floor off the coast of Hawaii.

The ocean floor has mountains and valleys. It also has one of the flattest places on Earth—the **abyssal plain** (uh-BIS-uhl PLAYN). The abyssal plain includes the vast flat lands beyond the continental shelf that cover almost half the deep-ocean floor.

The ocean floor has volcanoes, called seamounts. The Hawaiian Islands are seamounts that have risen above the ocean's surface. The sea also has mountain chains called midocean ridges.

The deep ocean floor is a diverse ecosystem. Many organisms at these depths rely on a shower of dead plant and animal matter for food. Many organisms live only on this "sea snow." Sometimes a dead animal, such as a whale, falls to the ocean floor and becomes food.

In 1977, two geologists made an important discovery near the Galápagos Islands. They found hot water **vents** at a depth of 3.2 kilometers (2 miles). The temperature in some of these vents was more than 371 degrees Celsius (700 degrees Fahrenheit). The water was full of minerals and bacteria. Giant tube worms also lived near these vents.

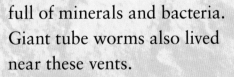
A hot, black smoker vent in the Gulf of California has been measured at 232 degrees Celsius (450 degrees Fahrenheit).

The **food chain** at these vents is based on chemosynthesis, rather than photosynthesis. Bacteria at the vents, not plants, produce sugars and other nutrients from sulfur compounds instead of from sunlight. The bacteria form the base of the food chain that provides energy for the vent animals. Since this discovery, hundreds of new species have been found living near sea-floor vents.

All of the ocean ecosystems provide many valuable resources for the countries of the world. Governments have begun writing laws to protect the oceans from pollution and overfishing. People have begun to understand how the ocean and its ecosystems affect all life on Earth.

Glossary

abyssal plain (uh-BIS-uhl PLAYN) the vast flat lands beyond the continental shelf that cover almost half the deep ocean floor *(page 21)*

adaptation (ad-up-TAY-shuhn) a characteristic of an organism that increases its chance of survival in an environment *(page 15)*

continental shelf (KON-tuh-NEN-tuhl SHELF) the underwater edge of a continent *(page 10)*

current (KUR-uhnt) an ocean movement; a large stream of water that flows in the ocean *(page 12)*

ecosystem (EK-oh-sis-tuhm) all the living and nonliving things in an environment, including their interactions with one another *(page 4)*

food chain (FOOD CHAYN) the path of the energy in food from one organism to another *(page 22)*

invertebrate (in-VUR-tuh-brayt) an animal that does not have a backbone *(page 8)*

photosynthesis (foh-tuh-SIN-thuh-sis) a food-making process by which green plants trap light energy to change carbon dioxide and water into carbohydrates (sugars) *(page 7)*

plankton (PLANGK-tuhn) organisms that float on the water in ocean ecosystems *(page 7)*

vent (VENT) an opening through which gas, liquid, or pressure escapes *(page 21)*

Index